200
KEYS TO UNLOCK
YOUR DESTINY

200
KEYS TO UNLOCK YOUR DESTINY

WALE OLADIPO

authorHOUSE®

AuthorHouse™
1663 Liberty Drive
Bloomington, IN 47403
www.authorhouse.com
Phone: 1-800-839-8640

First published by AuthorHouse   09/14/2011

ISBN: 978-1-4567-9716-4 (sc)
ISBN: 978-1-4567-9717-1 (ebk)

Printed in the United States of America

Any people depicted in stock imagery provided by Thinkstock are models, and such images are being used for illustrative purposes only.
Certain stock imagery © Thinkstock.

This book is printed on acid-free paper.

To my wife and children, Emma,
Daniel and Carys

Acknowledgements

Thanks to Emma for her input, encouragement and critique. My appreciation also to her parents, Malcolm and Trees Fewster, for their love, support and hospitality.

1. *Whatever you do daily grows to shape your future.*

2. *Never focus today on what you do not desire in your future.*

3. *Opportunities are concealed in every crisis, but they must be discerned.*

4. *Imagination is like a blank cheque; you can cash in whatever you dare to imagine.*

5.   *Your mind is like a goldmine; if you dig hard you will discover astonishing treasures.*

6.   *Love is the incorruptible seed that produces uncommon harvests in any environment.*

7.   *A positive attitude will take you further than genius.*

8.   *Uncommon success never strolls into your life; it arrives at the speed of your diligence.*

9.   *Analyze your disappointments long enough to dig out the wisdom hidden within.*

10. *People skills matter; without them, inappropriate people become your companions.*

11. *Dialogue is an indispensable seed for reconciliation.*

12. *Your mind has a mandate to focus on the positive, but the choice is yours.*

13. If you camp too long among losers, you will soon forget what winning feels like.

14. Whatever you are unwilling to unwind remains twisted.

15. Love is held captive to your mind until your heart gets involved.

16. The battle of life has no neutral ground; you are either winning or losing.

17.   Friends are not just companions; they are agents for your success or failure.

18.   People will only seek your wisdom, not your foolishness.

19.   Your greatest fulfillment and satisfaction in life will come not from what you receive, but from what you give.

20.   Your times in the valley of life are equipping you for your mountain top survival.

21. *Healthy obsessions are seeds for success.*

22. *The proof of wisdom is the willingness to learn.*

23. *Painstaking preparation is the secret weapon of champions.*

24. *You will always be courted by ignorance and obscurity in a subject in which you have no interest.*

25. *Imagination is the eye of the mind; the genius of the mind remains paralyzed until it sees through your imagination.*

26. *You will never fight a greater battle on the earth than the battle of the mind.*

27. *It is not what you are that matters most, but who you believe.*

28. *Until you become wiser than your enemies, your peace is subject to their moods and movements.*

29. Create a huge masterpiece in your mind of your future successes until you block out the postcards of your past failures.

30. Your life will always attract the fear your mind grows over time.

31. Don`t resign yourself to failure; prepare for victory.

32. Never deploy your prayer language for a battle that can simply be won by taking to your heels.

33. *Every exceptional achiever knows the importance of accessing the mind of another.*

34. *If you still harbour reasons for being dishonest, you have not fully repented.*

35. *It is prudent to learn from the past; it is imprudent to live there.*

36. *Labour for discernment; good timing hosts the beauty of everything.*

37. *Never trivialize the importance of financial blessing. Money is a seed to create positive changes in the world around you; thousands of children die daily of diseases that money can cure.*

38. *Habit is a gift, not an enemy, when deployed positively to fulfill your dreams.*

39. *Right words do not necessarily denote a right spirit.*

40. *Any foolishness left unchallenged multiplies.*

41.   *God will always use what you already have to create your miracles.*

42.   *Never conclude that your life is destined for misery; nothing is as certain as change.*

43.   *Praise is a supernatural weapon for deliverance.*

44.   *Until people feel your heart of kindness, your influence upon them remains capped.*

45.   Your understanding of your divine right as a believer is vital to your success.

46.   Jealousy is a dangerous emotion, capable of stripping you of your kingly anointing.

47.   Your future is decided by who you listen to.

48.   One of the purposes of money is influence; some people are deaf to everything except money.

49. *Every miracle is preceded by a divine instruction. Therefore listen carefully.*

50. *Unpunctuality is an explanation of your level of passion.*

51. *No relationship keeps you where you are. If it is not increasing you, it is decreasing you.*

52. *If you come to Jesus for healing, stop analyzing your symptoms and doubting His medicine. Just trust the Great Physician.*

53. *You are as wealthy as your wisdom, but you can still decide to stay poor.*

54. *Someone who jeopardizes truth to gain your friendship is also capable of cooperating with your enemies.*

55. *Humility and a repentant heart are necessary qualifications for divine empowerment.*

56. *Your inner conversations are as crucial to your victory as your spoken words.*

57. *Faith is the divine access into God`s unmerited favour.*

58. *Your credibility is not proven by experience, but rather by your track record of competence and reliability.*

59. *It is impossible to excel in a relationship with someone who does not agree with your priorities.*

60. *Your focus decides your fear or your faith.*

61. *Favour is a clue to divine positioning.*

62. *Whatever diminishes your authenticity is an enemy of your future.*

63. *Certain temptations can only be escaped by running away from them.*

64. *Perpetual lateness is unvoiced rebellion.*

65. *Your future is decided by what you choose to remember.*

66. *One of the qualities of greatness is the capability to rule over one's emotions.*

67. *Winners understand how vital it is to remain on the offensive, because that's where winning is decided.*

68. *Hope is built through knowledge, but faith is birthed when knowledge collides with trust.*

69.   *The object of your hope determines the success or failure of your enemies.*

70.   *Never develop a boastful attitude, except about the Almighty God.*

71.   *Ignorance is not just a disease, it is a destroyer.*

72.   *Your level of prosperity is relative to your obsession with and obedience to the word of God.*

73. *Contentment is not necessarily a lack of ambition; rather it could be an unshakable confidence in the blessing of the Lord that despises dishonest wealth.*

74. *A battle that promises no reward is an unnecessary battle.*

75. *Ensure you are filled with the right Spirit, otherwise the wrong spirit will enter in; you are not designed to be empty.*

76. *The environments you permit decide what grows or dies within you.*

77.   *Your mouth isn't simply for talking and eating; it is also your deliverer.*

78.   *A sign of chronic ignorance is when truth is interpreted as blasphemy.*

79.   *Pay attention to your faith; it is more precious than gold.*

80.   *Never pursue promotion, rather labour to lay hold of wisdom.*

81. *God is not persuaded by your tears, pains and needs; He is only moved by faith.*

82. *Kingly luxuries are never meant for fools, therefore get understanding.*

83. *Honour is an inevitable companion of the wise.*

84. *Your provision and healing are only guaranteed at the place of your assignment.*

85. *When you eliminate the wrong people from your circle, you birth new energy and see pictures of possibilities.*

86. *Faith shipwreck is impossible for a mind anchored to the word of God.*

87. *Never allow the foolishness of the past to advance into your future.*

88. *Bitterness is defiance to divine instruction.*

89. *Who you believe decides what you bestow unto others.*

90. *The knowledge of God is the key to divine treasures.*

91. *Depression is a drought of the mind caused by broken focus.*

92. *Righteousness is a divine tree that produces peace.*

93. *Your willingness to reach will obtain for you that which money cannot buy.*

94. *If you lack sound counsel, you will fall, regardless of who you are.*

95. *Prosperity becomes inevitable when you make the Holy Spirit your financial mentor.*

96. *Never trivialize the golden opportunity of being mentored. It is a shortcut to success.*

97. *There is no perfect peace without responsibility; it will require focus.*

98. *God never gatecrashes; He only shows up by invitation.*

99. *Never give what you are unwilling to release.*

100. *If you want to be significantly fruitful in life, you cannot afford to belittle your relationship with the Holy Spirit.*

101. Unforgiveness is a statement of ingrati tude towards God.

102. Show me a man who rules over his temper, and I will show you a man of strength and wisdom.

103. Your willingness to ignore the trivial is a portrait of your wisdom.

104. The word of God is a fertile soil where faith is nurtured and grown.

105. *Privacy is necessary until it begins to perpetuate your ignorance.*

106. *Many people are unaware of their own genius; only a wise and secure leader can salvage it from wasting away.*

107. *Nothing accurately measures levels of strength more than adversity.*

108. *One of the benefits of adversity is its capability to reveal who you really believe.*

109. *If you fail in life it will not be because you fall, it will be because you did not get back up and try again.*

110. *If those around you discourage you, be strong and encourage yourself.*

111. *If your supplication defies the will of God, a universe full of sacrifices cannot persuade God to answer you in the affirmative.*

112. *Humility is the seed for restoration.*

113. *Your future is shaped by your predominant reflections.*

114. *Never despise God`s invitation to intimacy; miracles are at stake. Prayer is your channel for divine intimacy and miracles.*

115. *Imagination is the seed for multiplication. Your mind will multiply whatever you consistently imagine.*

116. *You are only permitted to be childish when a child, not as a man.*

117. *Faith is the supernatural force that unleashes divine intervention.*

118. *The importance of any relationship is decided by its relevance to your passions.*

119. *Dishonesty is not only a photograph of character; it is also faithlessness in God's divine provision.*

120. *Whatever you give out, you will attract.*

121. *Never fight a battle today that is scheduled for tomorrow. Such is anxiety.*

122. *Your attitude is expressed in your reactions and your reactions determine the blessings you can access.*

123. *Fear is the consequence of broken focus.*

124. *The voice you trust decides your future.*

125. *Your dominant difference to another is the secret door to your life`s success.*

126. *Your belief system determines your decisions, and your decisions decide your destiny.*

127. *Passion without knowledge is deadlier than ignorance. It is like diving into a deep river without knowing how to swim.*

128. *Dishonour produces tragedy as surely as honour produces favour.*

129. *You are unqualified to harvest divine authority until you have learned to sow the seed of submission.*

130. *Your confession decides your conclusion.*

131. *The purpose of meditation is not to merge as one with the cosmos, but to renew your mind in the word of God.*

132. *Your self-image decides your behaviour.*

133. *Childlikeness is the seed for divine access, but childishness reveals little knowledge*

134. *The defeated trinity of the earth (the world, the flesh, and the devil) must always be regarded as such; defeated.*

135. *Whoever you habitually displease, you do not love.*

136. *Your destiny is never inevitable; it is a product of your decisions.*

137. *The proof of the indwelling of the Spirit is not in the dramatic, but in the demonstration of the Spirit`s fruit.*

138. *Your kindness will be remembered longer than your genius.*

139. *Your prosperity does not consist in your experience or qualifications, but in your obedience to the instructions of God.*

140. *Evaluate your ordeal until you eliminate any contributing foolishness.*

141. *Anything you disregard, you cannot attract.*

142. *Disorder creates pain, but order births pleasure.*

143. *Grumbling against God is an express ignorance of divine protocol.*

144. *Unforgiveness is a wisdom problem.*

145. *The memory of past victories is beneficial until it diminishes passion to reach for a greater future.*

146. *Past failures and disappointments are tutors that prepare you for your destiny; just make sure you are a good student.*

147. *You will never access your future beyond your willingness to let go of the past.*

148. *Reaching always precedes receiving.*

149. *Your destiny is simply your chosen place of arrival.*

150. *Your life's reward will be decided by your willingness and obedience.*

151. *Something of significance rarely turns up at your door by chance; it is usually the harvest of pursuit, passion and persistence.*

152. *The speed limit of your future is designed by God but decided by your thinking.*

153. *Obsession is the seed for mastery.*

154. *If you want to fulfill your destiny, you must know more than God; people skills matter immensely.*

155. *Bitterness is a destructive energy that flourishes in an environment of unforgiveness.*

156. *Don`t waste your time changing the mind of your enemies; it is an unnecessary battle.*

157. *Wisdom is the ability to solve human problems with the expertise of God.*

158. *Offense produces anger, but unforgiveness is a decision.*

159. *The strength of a man does not consist in his youthfulness, but in whom he believes.*

160. *Your decisions determine your destiny, not vice versa.*

161. *Your gifts, talents, skills and knowledge are precisely assembled for your assignment on Earth.*

162. *Success follows those who refuse to let life happen to them.*

163. *Doubts sabotage miracles.*

164. *Bitterness is a self-induced toxin capable of poisoning your sanity.*

165. *Humility is the prerequisite for promotion.*

166. *Life is a sequence of battles; strive to become an effective warrior.*

167. *The favour you respect and pursue is the favour you attract.*

168. *The wage of carelessness is mediocrity.*

169. *Until you are persuaded about your strengths, your weaknesses become your focus.*

170. *Your point of vulnerability is the target of the enemy.*

171. *Pride is to contest the sovereignty of God.*

172. *Strength and power belong to the knowledgeable.*

173. *Thankfulness is a magnet for unprece-dented favour.*

174. *Listening is an instrument which connects you to the pain of another.*

175. *The quality of your passion for God decides the quantity of His indwelling in you.*

176. *Gratitude is your statement to the giver that you have not taken his kindness for granted.*

177. *Your character is a photograph of your wisdom or lack of it.*

178. *A lifestyle of thanksgiving is only maintained by the persuaded.*

179. *Correction is proof that someone wants the best for you.*

180. *Be vigilant when your enemy makes peace with you; he may soon change his mind.*

181. *The word of God is an indomitable weapon by which your victory is guaranteed.*

182. *What you respect comes towards you.*

183. *Earnest expectation is the key to obtaining.*

184. *Worrying is to sack God as your helper, then give your confused mind the job.*

185. *Wisdom is the ability to distinguish between right and wrong.*

186. *Stay faithful in challenges; there is always somebody watching who is an agent for change.*

187. *Be firm with evil people; evil is not a spontaneous disposition but a philosophy.*

188. *Never fight the battle of life on your own; it is too exhausting.*

189. *When you increase in wisdom, you increase in favour.*

190. *Thanksgiving is proof of faith.*

191. *Listening is your bridge to the wisdom of uncommon leaders.*

192. *Seasons of your life can be dictated by those around you.*

193. *Whatever you are willing to live without, you will.*

194. *Experience is the slowest and most costly means of gaining wisdom; be quick to learn from the mistakes of others.*

195. *Financial prosperity is never a destination, but a tool to help accomplish your God-given assignment.*

196. *Nobody fully appreciates their blessings until they have experienced the contrary.*

197. *What you hear determines your energy.*

198. *Excellence is the seed for greatness.*

199. *Recognizing your assignment on earth isn't rocket science; there are three major signpost questions: what do you really love doing? What do you hate with a passion? What brings tears to your eyes?*

200. *With the blessing comes the responsibility to be a blessing to others.*

Appendix

Scriptural References:

1.	Proverbs 22:29	23.	2 Timothy 2:15
2.	Isaiah 43:18-19	24.	1 Corinthians 1:23
3.	Genesis 40:6	25.	Proverbs 23:7
4.	Ephesians 3:20	26.	Proverbs 4:23
5.	Proverbs 4:23	27.	Matthews 21:32
6.	1 Corinthians 13:8	28.	Psalm119:98
7.	Philippians 2:5-9	29.	Philippians 3:13-14
8.	Proverbs 22:29	30.	Job 3:25, Proverbs 29:25
9.	Romans 8:28		
10.	Proverbs 18:24	31.	Psalm 57:7
11.	Isaiah 1:18	32.	Genesis 39:12
12.	Philippians 4:8	33.	Proverbs 15:22
13.	Proverbs 13:20	34.	2 Chronicles 7:14
14.	Matthews 23:37	35.	Philippians 3:13
15.	Matthews 12:30	36.	Ecclesiastes 3:11
16.	Ephesians 6:12	37.	Ecclesiastes 7:12
17.	Proverbs 13:20	38.	Daniel 6:10
18.	1 Kings 10:24	39.	Acts16:17-18,Proverbs 26:25
19.	Acts 20:35		
20.	2 Corinthians4:17, 1 Samuel 17:40	40.	Ecclesiastes 10:13
		41.	Exodus 4:1-3
21.	Daniel 6:10	42.	2 Corinthians4:17, Romans 8:28
22.	Proverbs 9:9		

43.	Acts 16:25-26	67.	Ephesians 6:16-17
44.	1 Corinthians 13:4	68.	Psalm 9:10
45.	Jeremiah 29:11	69.	Psalm 20:7
46.	1 Samuel 18:8-9	70.	Jeremiah 9:24
47.	1 Samuel 18:7	71.	Hosea 4:6
48.	Deuteronomy 8:18	72.	Joshua I: 8
49.	Luke 24:49.	73.	Proverbs 10:22,
50.	Romans12:11		Ecclesiastes 4:6
51.	1 Corinthians 15:58	74.	1 Samuel 17:26.
52.	Matthews 9:23-24	75.	1 Samuel 16:14
53.	Proverbs 24:5	76.	Psalm 1:1-3
54.	Jeremiah 9:5	77.	Proverbs 12:6,
55.	Isaiah 57:15		Romans 10:10
56.	Matthews 9:21	78.	John 10:33-34
57.	Romans 5:2	79.	1 Peter 1:7
58.	Job 1:1	80.	Proverbs 4:8
59.	Amos 3:3	81.	Hebrews 11:6
60.	Psalm 112:7	82.	Proverbs 19:10
61.	Matthews 10:14, Psalm 5:12	83.	Proverbs 26:1
		84.	Exodus 23:25
62.	Psalm 1:1	85.	Genesis 13:14
63.	1 Corinthians 6:18	86.	1 Timothy 1:19
64.	Matthews 5:37, James 5:12	87.	Ecclesiastes 7:25
		88.	Ephesians 4:31
65.	Lamentations 3:21	89.	John 7:38
		90.	2 peter 1:3-4
66.	Proverbs 16:32	91.	Isaiah 12:3

92.	Isaiah 32:17	118.	2 Corinthians 6:14
93.	Isaiah 55:1	119.	Acts 5:3-4
94.	Proverbs 11:14	120.	Galatians 6:7
95.	Revelation 3:18	121.	Matthews 6:34
96.	2 Corinthians 1:24	122.	Number 14:24
97.	Isaiah 26:3	123.	Matthews 14:30
98.	Revelation 3:20	124.	Proverbs 1:33
99.	2 Corinthians 9:7	125.	Proverbs 18:16
100.	Isaiah 32:15	126.	Luke 6:34
101.	Ephesians 4:32	127.	Proverbs19:2
102.	Proverbs14:29, Proverbs 16:32	128.	Exodus 20:12
		129.	James 4:7
103.	Proverbs 19:11	130.	Hebrews 4:14
104.	Romans 10:17	131.	Joshua 1:8
105.	Proverbs 15:22	132.	Proverbs 23:7
106.	Proverbs 20:5	133.	1 Corinthians 13:11
107.	Proverbs 24:10	134.	1 John 4:4
108.	Habakkuk 3:17-18	135.	Romans 13:10
109.	Proverbs 24:16	136.	Proverbs 22:29
110.	Samuel 30:6	137.	Galatians 5:22
111.	Numbers 23:8	138.	2 Samuel 10:2
112.	Isaiah 57:15	139.	Joshua 1:8
113.	Proverbs 23:7	140.	Proverbs 18:21
114.	1 Thessalonians 5:17	141.	James 4:8
115.	Ephesians 3:20	142.	Proverbs 24:3-4
116.	1 Corinthians 13:11	143.	1 Corinthians 10:10
117.	Hebrews 11:32-34	144.	Proverbs19:11

145.	Philippians 3:13	171.	Daniel 4:24
146.	2 Corinthians 4:17	172.	Proverbs 24:5
147.	Philippians 3:13	173.	Acts 2:47
148.	Matthews 9:20	174.	Matthews 20:24
149.	Philippians 3:14	175.	Psalm 107:9
150.	Isaiah 1:19	176.	Psalm 103:1-3
151.	Proverbs 13:4	177.	Galatians 3:26-29
152.	2 Peter 1-9, Proverbs 23:7	178.	Habakkuk 3:17-19
		179.	Revelation 3:19
153.	Deuteronomy 6:6-9	180.	Exodus 14:5
154.	Romans 12:18	181.	Isaiah 55:11
155.	Job 21:25	182.	Proverbs 13:20
156.	Exodus 23:22	183.	Romans 5:5
157.	1 Kings 3:28	184.	Jeremiah 17:5
158.	Colossians 3:8	185.	1 Kings 3:9
159.	Isaiah 40:30-31	186.	Acts 27:43
160.	Joshua 24:15	187.	Psalm 64:4
161.	Exodus 31:1-6	188.	Ecclesiastes 4:9
162.	Proverbs 13:4	189.	Luke 2:52
163.	James 1:6	190.	Psalm 137:4
164.	Acts 8:22	191.	Luke 9:35
165.	1 Peter 5:6	192.	Gen 13:8-9
166.	Eph 6:10-13	193.	Heb 11:35, Matt 23:37
167.	Jude 1:21	194.	1 Corinth 11:1
168.	2 Peter 1:10	195.	Proverbs 22:9
169.	Psalm 139:14	196.	Lamentations 3:19-24
170.	Luke 4:2-4		

197.   *Job 4:4*

198.   *2 Peter 1:5-10*

199.   *Matthews 6:34*

200.   *Genesis 12:2*